Instructions for a Teenage Armageddon

Rosie Day

methuen | drama
LONDON • NEW YORK • OXFORD • NEW DELHI • SYDNEY

METHUEN DRAMA
Bloomsbury Publishing Plc
50 Bedford Square, London, WC1B 3DP, UK
1385 Broadway, New York, NY 10018, USA
29 Earlsfort Terrace, Dublin 2, Ireland

BLOOMSBURY, METHUEN DRAMA and the Methuen
Drama logo are trademarks of Bloomsbury Publishing Plc

First published in Great Britain 2024

Cover photo: Josh Shinner

Cover design: Desk Tidy Design

A catalogue record for this book is available from the British Library.

A catalog record for this book is available from the Library of Congress.

ISBN: PB: 978-1-3505-0226-0
ePDF: 978-1-3505-0227-7
eBook: 978-1-3505-0228-4

Series: Modern Plays

Typeset by Mark Heslington Ltd, Scarborough, North Yorkshire

To find out more about our authors and books visit
www.bloomsbury.com and sign up for our newsletters.

Instructions for a Teenage Armageddon was first performed at Southwark Playhouse on 9 February 2022, with Rosie Day originating the role of Girl. The cast and team below reflects the West End transfer, which opened on 17 March 2024.

Girl	**Charithra Chandran**

Video Cast

Mum	**Shelley Conn**
Dad	**Philip Glenister**
Ella	**Isabella Pappas**

Creatives

Writer	**Rosie Day**
Director	**Georgie Staight**
Set and Costume Designer	**Jasmine Swan**
Lighting Designer	**Rory Beaton**
Sound Designer	**Sam Glossop**
Video Designer	**Dan Light**
Production Manager	**Toby Darvill**
Producer	**Katy Galloway**
Associate Director	**Hanna Khogali**

Charithra Chandran – Girl

Charithra Chandran is a British Asian actress, producer and activist last seen in season 2 of Netflix's *Bridgerton* and Prime Video's *Alex Rider*. She will next be seen in Alex Sanjiv Pillai's romantic comedy *How to Date Billy Walsh* alongside Sebastian Croft and Tanner Buchanan. Charithra is also a global ambassador for Room to Read, a charity committed to providing books and literacy and practical skills programmes to children across the world.

Rosie Day – Writer

Author, film-maker and award winning actor Rosie has received major recognition for her brave, bold and honest artistry.

Instructions for a Teenage Armageddon opened to seven 5-star reviews and multiple OFFIE nominations at Southwark Playhouse and in February 2024 will have its European premiere in Sweden at Riksteatern.

Rosie's debut book of the same title was published by Hachette in 2021. Her sophomore non-fiction book *I Think I Like Girls* is to be published by Piatkus/Little Brown in 2025.

As a director, Rosie is currently directing feature film *The Shallow End* for Playhouse Studios and Simon Curtis, and is set to direct the feature adaptation of *152 Days* by Giles Paley-Phillips.

As an actor she has starred in film and TV series such as *Outlander*, *Living the Dream*, *Down a Dark Hall*, *All Roads Lead to Rome*, *Good Omens* and more. Theatre includes *The Fellowship* (Hampstead Theatre); *The Girl Who Fell* (Trafalgar Studios); *Again* (Trafalgar Studios); *Spur of the Moment* (Royal Court).

Georgie Staight – Director

Georgie is a freelance director working predominantly across new writing for stage and screen. She is an associate director at The Watermill and Mountview Academy of Theatre Arts.

Director: *Instructions for a Teenage Armageddon* (Garrick Theatre, original production at Southwark Playhouse nominated for four Off-West End Awards); *The Wizard of Oz, Camp Albion, A Christmas Carol* (Watermill Theatre); *Vinegar Tom* and *The Wind in the Willows* (Mountview); *Queen Mab* (The Actors' Church); *Things I Know To Be True* and *Our Town* (Royal Academy of Music); *Eigengrau* (Waterloo East Theatre); *D-Day 75* (Watermill Theatre, Greenham Trust and Corn Exchange); *Chutney* (Bunker Theatre, nominated for four Off-WestEnd Awards); *Into the Numbers* and *Dubailand* (Finborough Theatre); *Section 2* (Bunker Theatre); *Dreamless Sleep* (Arts Theatre); *Flood* (Tristan Bates Theatre).

Associate director: *Operation Mincemeat* (West End); *Dawn French is a Huge Tw*t* (West End and tour).

Assistant director: *Sweet Charity* and *Our Town* (Watermill Theatre); *Legally Blonde: The Musical* (Bernie Grant Arts Centre).

Jasmine Swan – Set and Costume Designer

Jasmine Swan is an award-winning set and costume designer working across theatre, opera, dance, live events and immersive experiences. Jasmine won Best Costume Design at the UK Pantomime Awards 2023 for *Beauty and the Beast* at Mercury Theatre, Colchester. She was a The Stage Debut Award Nominee in 2018 for Best Designer, for her debut season of work. She was a Linbury Prize for Stage Design Finalist in 2017 and has been nominated for multiple Off-West End awards. Jasmine was a resident designer at New Diorama Broadgate design studio 2021/22 and was Laboratory Associate Designer at Nuffield Southampton

Theatres in 2017/18. She is interested in creating surreal, abstract and expressionistic spaces, with sustainability and a greener practice in mind. She is a member of Scene Change.

Theatre credits include *The Big Life* (Stratford East); *The Full Monty* (UK tour); *House of Flamenka* (Sadlers Wells); *Beauty and the Beast* and *Sleeping Beauty* (Mercury Theatre, Colchester); *The House with Chicken Legs* (Les Enfants Terribles UK tour); *We Are As Gods* (Battersea Arts Centre and National Theatre River Stage); *The Narcissist* (Chichester Festival Theatre); *Recognition* (Talawa Studios, Fairfield Halls); *Lava* (The Bush); *The Jungle Book* (Watermill); *Eden* and *The Forest* (Hampstead Theatre); *Misfortune of the English* (Orange Tree Theatre); *Here* and *Shook* (Papatango at Southwark Playhouse); *Women in Power* (Nuffield Southampton Theatres and Oxford Playhouse); *Animal Farm* (National Youth Theatre UK tour); *Armadillo* and *SexSexMenMen* (The Yard); *Lady Chatterley's Lover* (Shaftesbury Theatre); *Sonny* (ArtsEd); *Little Shop of Horrors* and *Earthquakes in London* (LAMDA); *Scoring a Century* (British Youth Opera); *Son of Rambow* (The Other Palace); *The Tide Jetty* (Eastern Angles tour).

Rory Beaton – Lighting Designer

Rory is a freelance lighting designer working in the UK and internationally. He won Best Lighting Design at the Broadway World 2023 awards for *The Lord of the Rings*. He has previously been nominated for a Knight of Illumination Award for his work on Così fan Tutte at Opera Holland Park. He is also a recipient of the Michael Northen Award, presented by the Association of Lighting Designers.

Previous projects include *The Time Traveller's Wife* (West End); *The Lord of the Rings* (Watermill Theatre); *For Black Boys Who Have Considered Suicide When the Hue Gets Too Heavy* (Apollo, West End and Royal Court); *Death Drop: Back in the Habit* (Garrick, West End); *Jews. In Their Own Words* (Royal Court); *Merchant of Venice 1936* (Royal Shakespeare

Company and UK tour); *I Love You, You're Perfect, Now Change* (London Coliseum/Broadway HD); *Lovely Ugly City* (Almeida); Spike (UK tour); *Half Empty Glasses*, *A Sudden Violent Burst of Rain*, *The Ultimate Pickle* (Paines Plough); *Unexpected Twist* (UK tour); *Spike* and *Kiss Me Kate* (Watermill); *Dishoom!* (UK tour); *Summer Holiday*, *The Rise and Fall of Little Voice* (Bolton Octagon); *Edward II* (Arts Theatre, Cambridge); *Macbeth*, *La Bohème*, *Elizabeth I*, *The Marriage of Figaro*, *Dido and Aeneas*, *Amadigi*, *Idomeneo*, *Radamisto* (English Touring Opera). West End Producer – *Free Willy!* (Cuffe and Taylor); *Merchant of Venice 1936* (Watford Palace/Home Manchester); *60 Miles by Road or Rail* (Royal & Derngate); *The Blonde Bombshells of 1943*, *Summer Holiday*, *A Christmas Carol* (Pitlochry); *70 Års Opera* (Danish National Opera); *A Christmas Carol* (Belgrade/Chipping Norton); *Little Women*, *L'amico Fritz*, *The Cunning Little Vixen*, *Così fan Tutte*, *L'arlesiana*, *Manon Lescaut*, *Le Nozze di Figaro* (Opera Holland Park); *Boat, The Best Day Ever* (Company 3).

Rory has also designed projects with Blenheim Palace and The British Library.

www.rorybeaton.co.uk

Dan Light – Video Designer

Dan Light is a video designer, working across theatre, musicals, and live events. Dan is a regular collaborator with FRAY Studio, working as an associate across *Bat Out of Hell*, *Back to the Future*, *Frozen* and *Vogue World London*. Dan is the recipient of the Lord Mayor's Prize (GSMD), The Paul McCartney Human Spirit Award (LIPA) and a 2022 Offies Finalist.

Toby Darvill – Production Manager

Production management: *Pride in London* (London); *The Sound of Music* (Estonia); *Blockchain World Conference* (Abu Dhabi); *The Mountaintop* (UK tour); *Guys and Dolls, Oklahoma*,

Sweeney Todd, *Legally Blonde* (Wycombe Swan); *Cats* (Cyprus); *Beauty and the Beast* (Fereham Hall); *Hansel and Gretel* (Chiswick Playhouse); *HAIR* (London Vaults); *Bananaman* (Southwark Playhouse).

Hanna Khogali – Associate Director

Hanna is a British Arab creative, originally from the Midlands. She graduated from drama school in 2018, having previously studied at Durham University. Most recently she was assistant director on *The Wizard of Oz* at The Watermill. Hanna has also worked extensively as an actor. Theatre credits include Paines Plough's *You Bury Me* (Bristol Old Vic, Orange Tree); *Britannicus* (Lyric Hammersmith) and *Once* (UK tour).

Producer – Katy Galloway Productions

Katy Galloway is an independent theatre producer and lead producer behind Katy Galloway Productions.

West End productions include *Chess the Musical in Concert*, *Kinky Boots in Concert* and *Treason the Musical in Concert* (Theatre Royal Drury Lane); *The Last Five Years* (Garrick Theatre); *Wonderville: Magic and Illusion* (Palace Theatre); and *One Jewish Boy* (Trafalgar Studios).

Other theatre productions include *Treason the Musical* (UK tour); *Duck* (Arcola Theatre); *Smoke* (Southwark Playhouse); *Instructions for a Teenage Armageddon* (Southwark Playhouse); *Little Women* (Park Theatre); *Treason the Musical in Concert* (Cadogan Hall/Online); and Fringe First Award winning play, *Bobby and Amy* (Edinburgh Fringe).

Katy has also worked in producing and general management roles with companies such as Mark Rubinstein Ltd, DEM Productions and Chalk Line Theatre. She is currently working at Carter Dixon McGill Productions Ltd as producer and general manager across their slate including *Blippi: The Wonderful World* (UK tour) and *Death Note the Musical* (London Palladium and Lyric). Previously in her role at Mark Rubinstein Ltd, she worked as production assistant on *Tina: The Tina Turner Musical* (Aldwych Theatre); *Mandela* (Young Vic) and many other projects.

Katy has proudly worked with Stage One on their Commercial Producer Placement and on the Stage One/ Columbia New York Producers Exchange.

Instructions for a Teenage Armageddon

'' Denotes the **Girl** *playing different characters.*

Sensible Scout Leader Susan*'s dialogue can be heard as a voice over.*

Video footage is projected and used for her memory, the play can be performed with or without this.

Musical and cultural references can be updated to each production.

Lights up on a teenage **Girl**, *a live feed recording her.*

Girl Triskaidekaphobia.

Does anyone know what that means?

Fear of the number thirteen.

Of all the things I could fear

I'm scared of a number.

In ancient cultures thirteen was unlucky because it corresponded to the number of lunar or menstrual cycles in a year.

The theory is that, the number thirteen became cursed because it represented femininity.

Of course it fucking did.

My reason?

I was thirteen when my sister died.

It was a Yorkshire pudding that did it . . .

It's a complex carb.

She looks at the audience ruefully.

Mine burnt the inside of my mouth and I really don't understand why the things I love keep hurting me.

Sunday lunch,

She didn't want to eat it. And we all knew if she did put it in her mouth, she'd only throw it up ten minutes later.

Seemed like a waste of a perfectly good Yorkshire pudding if you ask me.

The trick to a good Yorkshire pudding is whatever the recipe, fling in an extra egg white.

Makes them blow up like balloons.

I should know.

I made them.

They taught us at Scouts.

A voice over plays out of her laptop from **Sensible Scout Leader Susan**.

Sensible Scout Leader Susan (*V/O*)   *For your Chef Activity Badge – Brian take your socks out of the microwave, I know it's the best way to dry them but take the beans out first – To pass your badge you must presents six perfectly formed Yorkshire puddings.*

Girl   Now I don't know if that was true

Or if Sensible Scout Leader Susan

Had been watching too much Master Chef.

But mine were really good.

Seeing as I made the Yorkshire puddings

Does that mean I killed her?

Imagine me in jail, and my new hefty cell mate asking what I'm in for:

'Killed someone mate'

'What with? Gun? Knife?'

'Nah, a more advanced pancake'

It's been four years and I haven't had them since.

Which is a real shame.

Everyone knows they're the best thing about a roast.

Because it wasn't *technically* the Yorkshire pudding that killed her, she didn't choke or anything, nothing that dramatic.

She just: dropped down dead.

In the middle of a blazing row about my fluffy, fatty, little parcels, her heart gave in.

Stopped.

Six years of anorexia will do that to a person.

Olive.

Seventeen years old just, gone.

Her name was Olive.

I know.

What's in a name eh?

I still can't sit down for Sunday lunch.

Sensible Scout Leader Susan (*V/O*)   *Local Knowledge Activity Badge, does everyone have an A to Z? What do you mean 'What's an A to Z?' A map Jenny!*

Girl   They went back and forth over what to do with her.

The body.

What she would have wanted.

Like she's DEAD guys I don't think she's too fussed.

I sat in the back seat of our car, my side, always on the left, peering out the window.

The sat nav was broken so

I was in charge of directions

That Mum made me print off the computer

Like it was 2002

Because the funeral parlour didn't come up on her phone.

A video of **Mum** *and* **Dad** *plays.*

Mum   But what if it's not what she wanted? I mean I never thought to ask?

Dad   Why on earth would you?

Mum   As a mother you're meant to know these things. Inherently.

Dad   You're meant to know her favourite band and bubble bath. Not whether she wanted to be cremated or buried.

Girl   Isn't it weird that there aren't dead birds everywhere? Like there's so many of them in the sky but I only see the odd one squashed on the road? Like where do they all go to die?

Mum   Are you paying attention?

Girl   Are *you* paying attention?

Dad   Knew we should of got that sat nav fixed, printing off directions feels prehistoric now.

Girl   Very 1989.

Dad   How would you know?

Girl   I don't. Taylor Swift might.

Dad   Can you stop trying to bring her into every conversation?

Girl   Only if you stop talking about golf.

Girl   LEFT, TURN LEFT, NOW, NOW!

Mum   You have to give me more warning than that!

Girl   OMG you're going the wrong way!

Dad   You said left!

Girl   I meant the other left!

Mum   That's RIGHT!

Girl   Well I don't know do I?!

Dad   I thought you were meant to be good at this – all those Scout hikes we bloody pay for.

Girl   I didn't think now was a good time to tell them

If they thought I was using a compass and the sun

For directions

When Google Maps was a thing

They were seriously delusional.

We were going round the North Circular

And Mum started crying.

We'd already lost her once,

And now we *literally* couldn't find her.

It was like a treasure hunt

Only the prize isn't buried treasure

It's burying your child.

Mum ran over a pigeon and I asked her whether it was best of three.

Video of **Dad** *plays.*

Dad   HOW IS THIS HELPING?

Girl   Eventually we found the road.

Old people's home, doctor's, funeral parlour.

And I thought . . . that's convenient.

They can just roll you from one to the next.

The funeral director looked like a mole

And spoke in a hushed sombre tone.

'I'm sorry for your loss, tea, coffee?'

I wondered if he always spoke like that?

'I would like sweet and sour pork, a chicken chow mein and egg fried rice'

He took us through the packages

We could have for Olive

Selling them like they were holidays.

'With this package we'll throw in the coffin for free'

Which I thought was really generous because

They are *expensive*.

And I'm pretty sure this funeral is eating into my university fund.

Can't we just bury her in the garden?

I sat scuffing my trainers on the funeral parlour floor wondering if they had a spare coffin for me to climb in and suffocate.

Got me thinking though.

What I'd want.

When I die smother me in garlic butter and toast me under the grill.

I fucking love garlic bread.

Moley the funeral director discreetly tries to ask how Olive passed away.

Beat. The **Girl** *waits.*

'Anorexia'

And I feel it build up inside me and I can't stop myself:

'Least the coffin'll be light'

'Dad, least the coffin'll be light'

DAD

DAD

DAD

Nothing.

Tough crowd.

Moley said that when someone dies,

You have to pick what to dress them in.

Hair, makeup, the works.

Like it could actually be like some bad BBC3 make over show hosted by Stacey Dooley.

It reminded me me of when we were little,

Mum booked one of those family photo shoots

With a photographer that spends his whole life

Photographing children in his basement,

And we got to wear sparkly lip gloss and green eye shadow
. . .

There's a photo hanging in our hallway,

Just me and her,

Arms round each other,

And I'm looking up at her, beaming,

So proud.

We settled on pyjamas.

I wanted her to be comfy.

She was going to be lying there for a very long time.

The day Mum took the clothes to the funeral parlour I came down for my daily bowl of Coco Pops,

and she had the pyjamas she'd chosen in her arms.

Only.

They were MY fucking pyjamas.

'MUM!'

'Don't!'

'But –'

'Don't be selfish –'

'BUT THEY'RE MINE!'

'None of hers fit her anymore'

That's Mum for you. Making sure her children are dressed properly. Even when they're dead.

I got them for my twelfth birthday.

Olive bought me a karaoke machine, she was really sick,

but that night, I put on all my birthday presents like you're obliged to, to show how much you

like them:

coat, pyjamas, hat,

And we sang Britney Spears so loudly the neighbours complained.

*'Toxic' by Britney Spears starts to play. The **Girl** dances one half of a double act dance routine, alone. It is clear she is dancing with someone as she sings.*

But I didn't want her to have my pyjamas.

That was my memory.

I get to keep something don't I?

Dad just sits behind his paper not saying a word, but I can see his fingers grip and crinkle the

paper tighter and tighter.

I read an article once, about a syndrome, where everyone, even doctors think you're dead.

Only you're not.

You're still alive, trapped inside your mind.

But no one can tell. So they bury you.

Terrifies me.

I use to tell Olive that if I ever died I wanted to be buried with my phone fully charged, switched off, buried not too far underground so I still get phone signal, so like, I could call her if I woke up and she could come dig me out.

I told Moley I wanted the same for Olive and

He laughed.

So I threw a stapler at him.

Sensible Scout Leader Susan *is singing 'Kumbaya' which leads into My Faith Activity Badge.*

Girl   The day rolled around.

Mum had been up all night making sandwiches and cake for the after party.

The wake!

Sorry, the wake?

Weird name for something celebrating someone who is definitely not awake.

I showered watching the water stream off my body thinking if I stayed in the shower. In this room. Forever.

Would anything even exist outside?

Thirteen is young for an existential crisis.

She'd laid an outfit on my bed:

A black pinafore dress that's too tight under my armpits cos Mum hasn't noticed I've grown since I was nine. Because she'd been busy with . . .

We weren't a religious family, but funny when someone's dead or dying you automatically start praying, really hard, as if a life time of non-believing might be made up for by some really intense worshipping and get us a slot in the church.

It worked.

Two weeks after Olive died

Just before the funeral

We had a discussion about faith

At Scouts,

I withheld under grounds

That I thought religion was dangerous

As it seemed to cause every war in the world.

Sensible Scout Leader Susan said faith doesn't always mean religion

You can have faith without being religious

I didn't have the heart to tell her

I'd lost all faith in everything at that current moment in time.

Susan said had I ever thought

About reincarnation

I said yes

I have an irrational fear

That I'm going to come back

As a fish that hates water

And spend my life being cold.

'I meant for Olive? If she could come back as anything, what would it be?'

'Me'

'Come on now'

'Skinny Susan. She'd come back as Skinny'

I watched the coffin be carried down the aisle,

and to be fair, they were doing a really great job of making it look heavy.

Mum had asked for so many candles to be lit, it looked more like a seance than a funeral.

Olive believed that we're born with all these little flames, these magical little lights inside us – full of joy and wonder and then life comes along, with it's troubles and pain, and one by one they get put out.

Guess all of hers went out.

Mum let me pick a song to be played.

'Any?'

'Any.'

I picked 'Come on Eileen'.

The first chorus of the song 'Come on Eileen' by Dexys Midnight Runners plays from 'Come on Eileen . . .' to '. . . in that dress, na na na'.

The crying got louder.

There's something really unsettling seeing your parents cry.

Defeated.

I didn't though.

I just stood there and thought

She looks up to the sky.

'You Fucker'.

Sensible Scout Leader Susan *(V/O)   Educational Studies Badge. 'Educating the mind without educating the heart is no education at all' was not said by Rihanna, Jane.*

Girl   When school found out, I was essentially a leper.

The stares, like a car crash,

except, I'm not the victim.

I'm still me.

I had friends, before, but like, no one knows what to say to you when someone

dies, so they just sort of . . . stop saying anything at all to you.

I *planned* not to tell anyone.

First few days just kinda got on with it.

But then it was in the paper.

And I could do that thing of going around every newsagent's in a five-mile radius and destroying all of them

but my legs are short,

and school starts at eight.

And then there was THE assembly.

Old Mr Cates,

age never disclosed but possibly fought in World War Two,

Shuffles across the stage and stands at the lectern:

'Now, I have some very sad news to report

Many of you will know Olive Wilson, who was one of last year's leavers,

As some of you may have read this morning,

Olive sadly passed away at the weekend'

And I swear people gasp.

Two hundred heads turn like a shoal of gawping surprised fish.

Glaring.

'And we as a community offer our sincere condolences and deepest sympathies to her family at this truly difficult time.

Now on to the match reports, Year 9 girls had a successful tournament this weekend'

Because that's the natural progression from a death statement, hockey.

And I'm just sat there like . . .

She shrugs.

And I can see people are mad

At me

For not saying

Just

I didn't want the tag.

There's a girl a row in front of me

Actually crying,

Like sobbing

And at first I'm like,

sorry are we related or something?

Cos

It's OK

I'm fine.

Not fine.

But fine.

I put my hand on her shoulder,

Tell her not to get upset.

Olive wouldn't have wanted this,

Which is a flat out lie

Cos Olive would have loved this kind of dramatic display of attention.

And I'm comforting her

Thinking

I'm pretty sure you didn't even know her?

But if you want the grief

You can have it.

I've learnt that

people love to attach themselves

To drama,

So they feel as if they're part of something

'I'm so sorry,

My mother's brother's cousin's husband's sister's dog died last night

And it's really hit me hard'

So if you want to make this all about you

Then by all means . . .

Cos I don't want it . . .

Everyone thought I was mental for pretending it just hadn't happened.

At lunch time they'd watch me eat my dinner,

just checking,

as if I was genetically prepositioned to get it

One evening, about a year after she'd kicked the bucket,

We were having dinner

Together

As a family

Which

We'd not done

Because none of us wanted to set the table

For three

Not four

Because the more we can pretend she's just off on a gap year

The better.

Very British.

They were eating,

I was pushing pasta around my plate,

And I wasn't *not* eating,

it was just really average spaghetti.

And I'd sunk two Wagon Wheels after school.

I feel their gaze fall on me.

Concerned glances exchanged

And Dad grabs my wrist and points in my face

'I am not going through this again *with you*'

I didn't have the heart to tell him that if I was going to kill myself,

anorexia seemed like a very long-winded way to go about it.

A girl in my class

Catherine was so scared of catching it,

she started eating two bowls of cereal before bed.

She got fat.

PE sucked,

Science sucked,

anything that required a partner essentially . . . sucked.

And I am really good at science,

so god least pity me and do it to copy my answers?

Anyone?

suddenly my French oral exam on my family became

Je suis un enfant unique.

No et.

no and.

Just done.

Must be weird going from two to one.

They must think 'Oh god best look after the other one or we'll look like really shit parents if they both kick the bucket'.

Still.

Cost Effective.

Sensible Scout Leader Susan (*V/O*)   *Tom, he can't breathe if you put the bandages over his mouth, this is your Emergency Aid Badge.*

Girl   On a rare occasion they looked up from their work, they became worried I wasn't mixing properly.

Olive always had people round the house.

The last person I had round ran home crying because I showed them the spot where Olive dropped down dead.

As if all the girls in my class pretending I literally didn't exist was somehow my fault.

Before I was always Olive Wilson's little sister, but now I got a rebrand that I didn't even ask for . . .

I didn't mind cos I still had . . .

Scouts.

She takes off her hoodie to reveal a Scouts shirt.

In a damp school hall at six every Thursday I went and sat on a prickly plastic chair and learnt how to knot, sew, build a fire and help the elderly with all of society's socially inept misfits.

You'd think you'd have to give teenagers more of an incentive than a felt badge to do ANYTHING. But turns out you don't.

And it's competitive. Who can earn the most badges.

One week we're earning our first aid badge. Teaching us CPR.

And I can't help but think CPR . . . bit fucking late for that.

Could have been really useful two years ago.

And we're taking it in turns to do chest compressions on the dummy,

And when the boys have a go, they start messing around. Touching it. Essentially molesting it.

And I start to get upset.

Really upset. In a way I haven't for ages. The burning in your throat, can't swallow, heart sore kind of upset.

So I kick them out the way and get down on the floor and cradle the dummy, and whisper, it's all OK.

I've got you.

It's all OK.

And I know I'm looking bat shit crazy right now, I mean the thing's not even got any legs, but I'm cradling it like it's . . . Like it's . . . her.

And I can hear them, all pissing themselves behind me.

I run to the toilets and slam the door so hard I think the walls might fall in.

Sensible Susan, knocks on the door.

'Sweetheart, are you OK? Are you going to come out now? The boys have said sorry, but you know how it is boys will be boys'

Boys will be held accountable for their actions.

Sometimes.

Maybe.

'It's OK you know. It's all OK'

We lie to sad people, because we think it makes them feel better,

But sad people see through lies,

It's happy people you can trick with bullshit.

I don't come out.

She leaves.

I sit knees up on the toilet biting my knee.

A video of **Ella** *plays.*

Ella   You alright? You'll stink of piss if you stay in here too long

Girl   I climb from the toilet and pry open the stall.

Don't just stand there like a 'cripple' come on.

Noelle.

Ella, for short.

She's new to Scouts.

Perfect hair, flawless skin, and a cigarette constantly tucked behind her ear.

'Want to get out of here?'

I've still not spoken and I'm scared to in case all that comes out is hiccupy words.

And she is far too cool for me.

But she holds out her hand and we walk straight out the hall.

It's funny that, do anything with enough confidence and bolster and everyone just sort of lets you.

We sit in the woods behind the playground and she smokes.

'Thank you for, uh, for that'

'She speaks'

'Sorry I'm –'

'We all had you down as a mute'

'Yeah . . .'

Ella has a big sister, Gaia.

She's the same age as Olive.

Only, alive.

She offers me a cigarette.

I take it but don't actually inhale cos I'm scared I'll choke.

She asks what my game is.

I say Monopoly.

She laughs.

'You're the girl whose sister died, aren't you?

I really should get it printed on a t-shirt.

Sensible Scout Leader Susan (*V/O*)   *Fire Safety Activity Badge. Miriam, you need to leave the room for this you've got far too much Elnett on, you'll go up like the Wicker Man.*

Girl   But Ella's cool

She's the kind of girl

You never wash off

The way she sees the world

It sticks to you like

Like body glitter.

'It's not a tragedy

It's just life'

Things like that.

We sit in the park

After Scouts

Each week

And she teaches me to smoke.

I hate the way it makes my hair smell

But she looks so cool

And I want to look like that.

I feel like a foetus

Compared to her.

One week,

She invites me out

Friday night

With Gaia and her friend

Ben.

To a bar.

And I say

Sure.

Because she's the first person

Who doesn't make me feel like

A victim

or a saddo.

She says I wear my scars like a dress

And that the strength in that dress

Is really pretty.

And I think

You can tell a lot about a person

By what they choose to see in you.

Music kicks in. Montage of the bar plays behind her. She raises her voice to be heard.

It's loud.

And sweaty.

I feel the heat smack me in the face.

Big crowds

Make me nervous

I'm short.

'What do you want to drink?'

'UM . . . WHAT?'

'What do you want to DRINK?'

This is where I realise I don't know the names of any drinks.

Shit.

'Er . . . Vodka?'

'STRAIGHT? YAS GIRL'

She hands me a glass.

She takes a sip. Gasps.

IT TASTES LIKE PETROL.

I don't say that.

I say

CHEERS.

CHEERS.

CHEERS!

Gaia's friend Ben brings me over a cocktail.

'Thank you. No one's ever –'

'NO ONE'S EVER LIKE BOUGHT ME A DRINK
BEFORE'

'DRINK IT THEN'

Ben's fit.

Gaia says he's single

But doesn't know much about him

As they only ever meet to party

And extracting any information

Out of anyone when they're shit faced

Is harder than the Spanish Inquisition.

But I've seen this in movies

So I give it my best shot with Ben:

As the music cuts out awkwardly as she shouts:

'YOU LOOK LIKE A PIRATE WITH THAT EARRING'

Beat. Awkward moment. She slaps her head.

'FUCK!'

Ella grabs my hand,

And leads me through

The bodies of smiling people

Isn't it weird,

People are so much friendlier when

They're drunk.

Oh god.

She wants me to dance.

I can't dance.

Olive used to teach me routines

In our living room.

I'm not sure the Britney routine is the right thing to crack out here.

But Ella and Gaia and Ben

They're not even thinking

They're just free.

It looks fun.

So I slowly . . .

Slowly . . . join in.

She begins to dance.

Have you ever done that?

Tried to dance

And you feel really cool and great

And then you catch a glimpse of yourself somewhere And realise you look like a chimpanzee.

But when Ella looks up. She's staring at me. Grinning.

I think she can tell

I'm internally having a panic attack

Because the alcohol has really started to hit

And my whole body feels as if it's burning down.

And my mind's screaming 'EVACUATE, EVACUATE'

She pulls me on the floor,

Towards her,

To safety.

She puts her arms around my shoulders

'Let's be best friends forever'

She smiles a huge smile.

'Yeah.'

Sensible Scout Leader Susan (*V/O*)   *Billy! Billy! Drop the bow and arrow now! That is not how you earn your Master at Arms Activity Badge!*

Girl   When she was alive.

All they did was argue.

I spent hours

Leaning over bannisters

Ears to closed doors

I found a spot by the kitchen that if I crouched, I could see right through the door crack.

Watch them spit

Fiery verbatim

Back and forth

Triggering each other

Deliberately

With words to wound

Listening

To them shout

About her

About them.

And I hated it.

It became white noise.

In the background.

Constant.

There's only so long you can put a pillow over your face

Before you suffocate.

But after she died

I realised

Arguing's good

Arguing's great

We will take arguing!

Least they were willing to fight for something!

It's silence that's the fucker.

When there's no words left to say.

Or maybe there are,

They're just too poisonous to say out loud.

The house became quieter than a monastery.

Dad got up went to work.

Mum waited till he left.

Then off she'd go

Like a ghost leaving a trail of red wine behind her.

I'd wait for her to leave.

Then depending how I felt I'd drag myself out of bed.

Then we'd do the whole staggered routine in reverse in the evening.

I don't sleep.

We live in an old house and Olive and I shared a room in the attic.

We used to pretend it was our own flat.

Like one day we'd have our own place.

Together.

Now it's just me

rattling there empty.

And I'm scared.

I start this thing

Before bed

Of checking in every cupboard

On the top two floors

In case there's a kidnapper.

Waiting for me.

To which on bad days I might be like

Please take me.

I'm a willing victim.

I'd sleep in my dressing gown

Because I thought

If someone tried to stab me in my sleep

It'd be difficult to get a knife

Through my pink Marks and Spencer's dressing gown.

Logic.

They never even noticed.

Mum and Dad.

If they did

They never said anything.

Cos I didn't feel safe in their house.

They couldn't protect me.

They can't.

Fairground music begins to play.

One weekend,

Mum can't get out of bed so

Dad takes me to the fair.

Candy floss, hook a duck, those goldfish in bags that die after four hours, and a shooting gallery.

He's not one of those egotistical men

Who likes to prove their worth

And their manliness

By shooting things.

He's a police officer.

My aim's good

We did it at Scouts once

Archery,

But it got banned

Cos Billy Tomkinson

Shot a pigeon.

I load the pellets in the gun,

He puts his hands on my shoulders

She acts it out with darts and a dartboard.

Positions me.

I pull the trigger.

Bang.

'Mum and me . . .'

Bang.

'It's just . . .'

Bang.

'It's not'

BANG.

'We're getting a divorce sweetheart'

Bulls eye.

The fairground music stops.

I mean I'm not in the police but telling someone something shocking whilst they're holding a loaded air rifle doesn't seem like the most logical thing to do.

I almost took his eyes out.

So my life becomes a suitcase

I have no clean clothes

Because they each think

The other one is taking care of it.

I wash my pants in the sink.

I watch them try to be the more loved parent.

New phone off Dad.

Laptop off Mum.

They won't talk to me

But they'll buy me stuff.

Mum started dating again.

Pretty quick.

She did good.

Considering

She points to herself.

Baggage.

Enter Clive.

CLIVE.

The first time I met him,

Mum made me put on a dress.

And eyeliner.

Like Olive.

He sits on the sofa

And I swear

He licks his lips at me.

But he might be getting crumbs out of his disgusting moustache.

'Who's that then?'

What does Clive mean?

He's pointing to a framed photo of Olive by the TV.

'Olive'

'Who?'

'My sister'

She can't of –

'Oh there's two of you?'

She hasn't –

'She at uni?'

She hasn't fucking told him.

'She's dead Clive'

I stare at Mum who has found a very sudden interest in our beige carpet.

'Oh'

'Yeah. OH'

To this man,

She never existed.

And I leave.

Out the house

It's raining.

Hard.

But the drops are cold

And I like the way it feels.

Painful and alive.

I stand in the middle of the park

Arms out stretched

The sky just a blanket of grey.

And I'm kind of hoping can you drown from the rain?

I'm soaked.

I go into the park toilets

Metal

And

Muddy.

I look in the mirror.

The smudged kohl around my eyes.

The mascara down my cheeks.

My hair straggly and long sticking to my jaw.

My dress soaking and clinging to me.

And in that moment

I look like her

I see her.

I reach out and touch the glass –

Wishing I could break through.

'Olive –

'What's going on?'

I sit below the sink.

I don't want to go home.

Sensible Scout Leader Susan (*V/O*)   *Mathematics Badge, nine sevens are sixty – . . . has anyone got a calculator?*

A video of two young girls starts playing.

Girl   After she died.

We had a clear out

Cos you can't keep a dead girl's stuff forever.

And I found this file . . .

In it . . .

The video glitches.

Actually.

Sorry.

It doesn't matter.

Dad

Too.

He gets a new . . .

Woman.

Sarah.

I go round her house,

For the first time,

One of those pretty white brick

Three storey ones

That girls on Instagram

Pose outside of

Showing off their outfit of the day

As if making money out of what you wear

Is actually a thing,

Job description:

Coat hanger.

When I meet her

I'm taken a-back.

She's pretty.

Like beautiful.

And I'm like

Good on you man!

Weird to think anyone could EVER be attracted to your parents.

Dad has to leave for a night shift so it's just me and her.

Planned.

He tries to give me a hug goodbye,

Like that's something we do?

(We don't)

And I notice cuts on his arms,

He says they're from shaving

Like he's become one of those hairless metropolitan men who shave their arms?

Is this a mid life crisis?

Sarah say she's ordering a Domino's,

Asks if I like Britain's Got Talent.

I do

but only cos it makes me feel good about myself.

Schadenfreude.

Other people's shitty life making you feel good about yours.

Sarah and I sit at the counter,

It's awkward.

I feel myself talk in one-word sentences

Was I always this stoney?

Cos even I can tell I sound like a dick.

She says Dad doesn't talk about Olive really

Which is solid to know that if I bite the dust

My dad will erase me from his memory too.

A video of **Sarah** *plays.*

Girl   What has he told you?

Sarah   About you?

The girl shakes her head.

Sarah   Oh . . . about . . . If I'm being completely honest not a whole lot. I thought you could tell me about her?

The **Girl** *shrugs.*

Girl   Have you ever seen him cry?

Sarah   Only once. I came in here with his dinner and One Direction came on the TV.

Girl   Olive loved them.

Sarah   Did she?

The **Girl** *shrugs.*

Sarah   Well, he just broke down. It was a bit of a sight really. Your big old dad crying over Harry Styles.

Girl   I get the overwhelming feeling

To tell him

It wasn't your fault it wasn't your fault

It was . . .

It was . . .

She did it because of . . .

That's the thing about eating disorders

It's not just you.

It bleeds to everyone around you.

I tried to

Ignore.

But it does.

It gets in your bones.

An eating disorder via osmosis.

I realise I've been sat staring at the oven.

For five minutes

And not said a thing,

I mean Sarah's not even in the room anymore.

I hear a kerfuffle from the hallway.

And a voice.

A small tiny voice.

I scrunch my eyes and pray it not to be real.

No.

No way.

No way.

There in the hallway

In a red chequered summer dress

Stands a French plaited,

Gappy tooth ten-year-old.

Beat.

You've got to be kidding me.

Her name

Is 'Lottie'

I know this because

She screams it as

She throws herself

At me,

Sarah says

She's been excited to meet me all day

'Sorry it's not reciprocal

No one mentioned

Your existence'

She's got the face of a

China doll,

And the personality of a wet wipe.

She picks the toppings

And the cheese off her pizza

And nibbles the crust like a tiny rat:

'I scored the winning goal'

'In what? The World Cup?'

'Noooo, netball'

'It doesn't count though, does it, when the posts are only five foot high'

'And in maths I was the first to finish the question sheet and I beat all my friends, I have lots of friends'

'They'll desert you as you get older'

'Cleo and Beatrice and Seraphina and Sammy and Sebastian and Arabella –'

'And Prudence?'

'No she's in the year above, how do you know her?'

Jesus I have never been
So uninterested in my life.
Kids, they don't shut up do they?

'There's this girl at school called Lucinda,
who's always really mean to me
Mummy says to ignore her.
She used to be my friend
But then she started pulling my hair
And she stole my snack from my bag
Cos she doesn't like me anymore and
I don't know why'

'I think I can answer that one for you Lottie'

When it's time for her to go to bed,
Sarah, with her gleaming smile
Says
'Maybe if you ask nicely Lottie, she'll
Read you a bedtime story'
Like sorry what?
I'm not a ready made fucking baby sitter.
She's ten she can read it herself.

I lie awake in the spare room
Waiting for Dad to come home,
You know spare rooms,
That have never been finished properly?

People keep meaning to

But extra bills get in the way,

Or time runs away with itself

So it's half painted with temporary

Paint swatches

And has no curtains

Or carpets

And I'm definitely going to get a nail

In my foot and get sepsis.

I'm thirsty,

Cos dominoes without fail

Makes me need two litres of water

At about 2 am.

So I sneak out across the landing and I stop.

Pink lights glow from the room across from me.

Flashing, sparkly, dancing on the walls.

I slowly push open the door

To Lottie's room,

A pink princess palace

Adorned with ballet slippers

And teddy bears

And Barbie and Ken dolls

And Little Mix posters

And Lottie

Tucked up

In a tiny single bed,

Her long mousey hair

Flowing across the pillow.

As I get closer

I'm alarmed at how perfect she is.

How easy life must be

When you're ten and you look like that.

I just stand there

staring.

I bend down to examine

Closer,

And closer.

Her perfect little life

Unable to comprehend

The monumental shit show

She's been brought into.

I can feel her breath on my face.

I feel my hand clench,

My jaw lock.

And then she opens her eyes.

And screams.

Sensible Scout Leader Susan *(V/O)*   *Snapchat does not represent accurately the Communications Badge.*

Girl   It's Ella's fifteenth birthday,

We've been planning it for weeks,

And on Saturday we're wandering

round town for outfits.

There's this shop

Called Brandy Melville

That we love,

They have dresses like this film Clueless

That we watched.

Which was made like sixty years ago

But the fashion is so in right now.

But when we go try on the dresses

None of them fit Ella

Cos all clothes are one size only.

Which seems an extreme way

To filter who wears your clothes.

I tell her to screw them

And buy her her favourite frappuccino to cheer her up.

We're going to TGI Friday's.

Classic birthday meal.

Ella's friends from school are there,

But she wants to sit next to me.

'I think you're gunna need a bigger bed for this sleepover El'

'No – it's just you'

And I swear my heart could burst.

We cuddle close in bed,

As Ella regales tales of her

Boy of the week,

I can't keep up,

'What about Ben?'

'What about Ben?'

'You thought he was cute'

'Noo . . .'

I feel myself go red.

Damn my face betraying me.

What kind of evolutionary tool is blushing?

Ella makes me follow him on Instagram

But we realise in most of my pictures I'm dressed in school uniform.

So we take some more.

The **Girl** *acts out getting the perfect selfie, it is elongated and entertaining.*

'Ugh I wish my skin wasn't so bumpy'

'There's an app for that'

'I wish my eyes were bigger'

'There's an app for that'

'I wish my cheeks were more like more cheekboney'

'There's an app for that'

We post a black and white one

With me looking slightly bored

Like I'm not that interested in life.

I wake up the next day

And he's liked all of my pictures.

I really hope he understands how much trouble he's caused
for a girl he's only met once,

just by double tapping those photos.

So I message him,

'Alright, I get that you think I'm hugely photogenic'

and that's how it started.

Messaging back and forth,

all day every day.

Where you don't want to check your phone in case he hasn't
replied to your message,

but desperately hoping he has.

I like the way my name sits on his lips.

And he's nervous around me.

Dad says it's a good sign.

'Anyone that's too smooth around you.

Run.

The right person should be nervous

Enough to want to impress you'

Dad's prying into my love life

During a trip to PizzaExpress

Simultaneously classy and cheap

At the same time.

It almost feels like we're a family.

Sarah, Dad, spawn of satan Lottie and me.

Despite me ignoring her

At every possible

Occasion

Lottie

Will not

Let up:

'I came first in my gymnastics competition'

'Good for you'

'I'm dressing up as Tinkerbell for Halloween'

'Whoopdee fucking doo'

'I made you a bracelet in art'

'Don't want it'

'Lucinda kicked me in the shin today'

'LOL'

'I think your daddy loves me more'

The sun's going down

And the High Street's

Glowing a sort of rose tinted hue

And Ben's texting me

Flanter.

Flirty banter.

The jokes are easy,

The pizza's average.

And for the first time

In a long time

I feel

Hopeful.

But once we finish

Eating

I see Dad

Getting nervous

Keeps tapping

His fingers on the table

In a rhythm

And glancing over at Sarah

And I'm like

WHO'S DYING.

Come on fess up

I can take it.

'No one's dying sweetheart

Your Dad,

And I,

we're,

We're

Engaged

do you want desert?'

WHAT

'Brownie looks good'

WHEN

'Last week'

'I was there, Daddy gave Mummy a ring'

'He is *not* your dad'

'We didn't tell you before

Because we didn't want you to get upset'

'Oh yeah as you can see I'm delighted

Sarah you bitch.'

'Watch it'

It's his

I'm warning you voice.

I push back my chair

knocking my water off the table

hoping it sends shards of glass into

their shins.

I phone Ben

And there's something

About his voice that calms me down.

'People get engaged

All the time

It doesn't mean anything'

Dad comes out on to the High Street.

Like a sheep in very bad plaid clothing.

'Sorry love.

I wanted to tell you earlier but Sarah thought . . .

Miscommunication eh?

I'm sorry'

He means it.

'Come on, you're a big girl now'

'I'm not'

'It's a fresh start,

We'll be a family'

We had a family Dad.

'It'll be good for me'

I know it will.

I know that's what he needs.

I can see it.

But,

But,

'But what about me?'

Sensible Scout Leader Susan *(V/O)   Healthy Relationships*
Badge unlike my twelve-year marriage . . .

Ben lives in Brighton.

At the university.

After a while of

Obsessive texting,

He invites me down for the weekend.

'No'

I mean he's probably too old for me.

'Come on'

'I don't think so'

I've never asked

How old

Cos that's rude.

And I don't want him to think I'm a kid.

'Please come –'

'Oh alright then'

I immediately phone Ella

Who squeals a sound only mice can hear

And demands we go shopping

IMMEADIATLEY.

'Dungarees and a jumper with a cat on,'

'What are you a child?'

Yes.

'I know but you don't want to show him that'

As she's zipping me into a red

Bodycon dress that's

Crushing my ribcage

'IT'S PERFECT'

It is

If I don't want to ever breathe again.

'Do you have sexy underwear?'

I think about the pants I'm wearing

That still have the days of the week on.

'Why, he's not going to see –'

'The less clothes you have on, the better'

Which panics me.

Cos no one's seen me naked

Since.

Since Olive and I use to share baths.

'My pants are fine.

If they were fine for Bridget Jones

They're fine for me.'

We meet up with Gaia

'I think this'll be good for you'

She says

Grasping my cheeks in her hands.

And she gives me a hug

Her hair brushing my face

And I breathe in this sort of

Musty sweet perfume.

And if I close my eyes tight enough

I can pretend just for second

That it's . . .

Her.

I tell Mum I'm staying at Dad's

They don't speak to each other anymore

So they'll never check.

Mum offers me a lift to the station

We sit in the car

Silently

Rolling along.

She turns the radio on

Because the silence is deafening

The opening lines to the song 'Hey Mickey' by Toni Basil blare through the speakers.

I slam the radio off.

'You love that song'

'I used to'

Keep up Mum.

I wish I could talk to her about it.

I can't remember the last time I told her anything.

Or spent any time with her.

If people didn't react so dramatically to things,

If I knew I wouldn't get told off

I'd probably talk about it.

Things are going well for Mum and Clive,

But I don't think he likes me around,

My presence upsets Mum who'd rather pretend she was childless now.

He's the sort of man whose

Temper's so loud you feel it vibrates in your ribs,

The kind that makes you want to shout back,

But you're not allowed to voice an opinion at my age.

Even a valid one.

So you better keep your mouth shut.

The train leaves the station

and I'm sat there going

'This is mental, this is mental, what the fuck, who travels all this way to see someone they hardly know' but like, he asked me six times

and he wouldn't of if he didn't want me there right,

right?

I put makeup on on the train,

a little more than usual to make myself look older

Like seriously there should be more female surgeons,

Forget open heart surgery

doing winged eye liner on a train going ninety miles per hour

Takes PRECISION guys.

I spill the little pot of powder everywhere and the woman next to me tuts

and I'm like

'IF YOU KNEW HOW NERVOUS I AM RIGHT NOW'.

And the train pulls in,

And my heart is attending a house rave

But it's too late to go back now.

'Be a grown up'

So I walk through the exit and I scan around, again and again looking for him,

And there's a sinking panic

Rising in my stomach

what if he's not coming.

What if he has stood me up.

and my heart's in my mouth

and I don't recognise anyone,

and I bite the inside of my cheeks

I feel the tears spring in my eyes and then suddenly from behind there's a soft

'Hello'

in my ear.

And there he is.

He picks me up and spins me round and all the anxiety in my body just melts away.

'You came, you actually came' he says.

And I look at him.

His baseball cap, covering the sweat on his brow, his ring on his knuckle.

He takes my bag and my hand and he leads me to the car.

And the whole journey he keeps stealing glances at me,

like I'm the shiniest star in the sky.

He takes me for lunch,

Next to the beach.

fish,

ugh,

but I want to seem sophisticated,

so I don't say no.

They bring out the fish and

It's got scales and eyes and tiny little teeth.

Like the eels from the Little Mermaid I use to cry at and hide behind the sofa from.

It's staring at me, like it knows.

It knows I'm lying, it knows how anxious I am,

It knows, it knows, it knows.

So I whack off its head and throw it to the sea gulls.

He thinks it's funny.

I'm just trying to run from an overly judgemental fish.

We bump into his friend James at the restaurant,

And he knows *exactly* who I am.

James is older than Ben and keeps looking down my tank top

Which I tug up into my armpits.

I decided not to tell Ben

About Olive.

Ella agreed

'Don't put him off

With a sob story'

But the more I sit there

The more I want to speak about her

What she'd think of him.

Warn him

That she'd beat him up

If he hurt me.

How if he fancied me

He'd of been besotted with her.

Everyone was.

there was this . . .

Luminosity about her.

People were drawn to this

Light

And I didn't mind

Watching from the outside

Because she was all mine.

We spend the afternoon on the beach.

His arm around my shoulder.

She shrugs uncomfortable.

And I realise the last time I was on a beach I was ten.

Cyprus.

All inclusive.

We arrived late and Mum shouted at Dad on the first night cos he'd spent our holiday money on hotel where ketchup had been squirted down the halls.

But in the morning we threw back the balcony doors, and it was, paradise.

I feel my eyes get all watery

so I run into the sea,

and it's so cold.

So biting.

The pain.

I love it.

I lie on my back and listen to waves crash around me and think, I'm a brain in a jar, I'm a brain in a jar, I'm a brain in a jar.

Wondering if I should start swimming out to sea

Like Esther Greenwood does in *The Bell Jar*.

It's not the happiest of existences when Sylvia Plath is your hero.

We go back to his flat and hang out.

His parents must be loaded cos he lives by himself

And his apartment is beautiful.

All high ceilings and marble.

We get ready for a party his mates are throwing.

I've brought the outfit.

He says I look . . . cute?

He looks me up and down.

For the first time

He is a lion

And I am a lamb.

It hurts.

Really really hurts.

I clench my teeth trying not to yelp.

And I'm thinking, how does anyone ever get enjoyment out of this? This is meant to be a fun activity? I've never felt pain like it.

But it's meant to hurt right?

You're first time, it's meant to hurt.

Lie back and think of England and all that.

'Get off me'

He stops.

He looks down.

And I'm thinking, but you're meant to bleed right? That's normal? Everyone says they bleed the first time.

He pushes me towards the bathroom and turns on the shower, the sudden noise shakes me.

And the red against the pristine white tiles.

It frightens me.

This is wrong right?

Is something wrong?

He lifts me into the bath and makes me shower off.

He gets a big white towel and wraps me in it.

He picks me up, and like a baby he carries me back to the room.

And I'm thinking, Not again, please not again.

My body can't take it.

I'm hoping I might pass out

I count to a hundred in my head to try and focus but I keep losing track.

I bite my hand and try not to cry.

I want to go home.

The next morning,

I wander into the kitchen.

Silence.

He asks if I like guacamole,

'YES'.

I don't.

Because he's so fucking millennial that anything can be fixed with an avocado.

I think he's going to kill me and bury my body in the forest.

When's the age when you're no longer deemed cute enough
to be searched for?

'How old are you?'

He looks up.

'What?'

'How old are you?'

My voice is squeaking.

'You said you went to the uni,

But your mates

Didn't seem like students'

'I do go to the uni'

Right

'Every day'

OK

'I teach in the psychology department

I'm twenty-seven'

The kitchen tiles

Stick to the bottom of my feet

And I can't move.

I pack my things

As I walk down the corridor

A girl

No,

A woman passes me.

I hover just long enough to see her

Get out her keys,

And enter his flat with a:

'Hiiiiiiiiii *babe*'

With all the belief she can muster:

Maybe it's his flat mate?

I walk

In the pissing rain

To the station

Pyjama top still under my hoodie.

It's Sunday so I have to change

Trains three times,

I have a bath

When I get home.

There are hand prints

On my wrists

And ribs.

Part of me is hoping

Someone will barge in

To the bathroom

And see them all.

The first chorus of the song 'Come on Eileen' plays in full.

But they don't.

Sensible Scout Leader Susan (*V/O*)   *Horticulture Activity Badge. Who's ready to get their hands dirty?*

Girl   I waited for someone to text me.

Ask how it was.

They didn't.

I thought he might call me to . . .

Expecting to

have millions of texts and voicemails

And instead I have

Nothing.

I send Ella texts.

They're left unread.

Desperately playing over in my head what

He might have told them.

When my phone finally pings,

My heart hits the roof

And I grapple for my phone

Like it's about to detonate.

But it's Lottie,

Sending me another love heart

Princess GIF and a request to play Wordle.

For FUCK sake.

So Thursday comes around and off I go.

Ella's in the Wendy house with a new girl

So I go over and say

Video POV of **Ella** *in the Wendy house.*

Girl   'Hey . . .'

Ella   'Hey'

Girl   'Where have you been? I've been texting you non-stop'

Ella   'I know'

Beat.

Girl   And you know when you can tell

Something's up

But neither of you want to say anything

So you just pretend everything's fine

And we talk about the weather

As if we're thirty.

We sit in the garden

Throwing kindling

On the crappy fire

We tried to make last week.

It's spitting

I plunge a stick

Into my hand –

To desperately stop myself from crying.

Neither of us saying anything.

'Why did you tell him you were eighteen?'

'I didn't'

'He says you did'

'Gaia didn't tell me he was double my age'

'So it's her fault? She's really fucking angry at you'

'But I didn't do anything –'

'It was just meant to be a date,

you weren't meant to sleep with him?

He's freaking out.

It's so irresponsible, he could get in serious

Trouble

For that'

'It wasn't like –'

'He says you begged him'

'No I never I '

'It's' just a bit.'

'What?'

'Slutty'

I feel tears spring in my eyes –

'Gaia's really angry at you

He could lose his job

If you told the wrong person that'

'I won't, I swear I won't'

'What am I meant to do?'

'I'm sorry, I'm really sorry'

'You had to go fuck it up, make it awkward for me'

'It's not, it's fine, everything's fine'

'It's embarrassing'

She throws her cigarette on to the kindling.

The fire starts to burn.

She's sat right next to me

But it's like she's already left.

'Please don't go'

'I'll see you around'

'Please . . .'

Beat.

Slut.

Slutty.

Which isn't a thing.

There is literally no such thing.

SLUT

SLUTTY

Slut is a way of stopping girls having as much fun as boys.

Because sex is for them.

Life is for them.

Right?

I sit there

Not realising I'm

I'm –

Scratching my legs,

Until I draw blood.

If anyone asks,

Which they won't

I'll tell them it was Lottie's

Very angry psychopathic bunny.

It's fine.

I like my own company.

It's better to be on your own.

Don't put your happiness in someone else's hands.

They'll drop it.

Every.

Single.

Time.

I started disconnecting.

I was coasting.

On the surface.

The periphery.

Just watching.

Life.

People.

Dogs.

Numb.

Silence is a form of communication

If anyone ever thought to listen.

And I started to think I was incapable of feeling anything at all.

Because all of this.

All of this.

It's just a lot . . . when you're fifteen.

I message Ella

Again and again

Until it's just me

Talking to myself

Why do people take sides?

How am I so . . .

Disposable?

Sensible Scout Leader Susan (*V/O*)   *Poetry Badge, no, no it has to rhyme or it's not a poem.*

Girl   Three weeks later,

It still hurts

I take a trip to the doctor

I have to sneak out as Lottie's off school cos someone threw a rounder's ball at her head.

The doctor

She goes to examine me,

And I make the noise of

A Jack Russell whose foot I stood on once.

I watch her concerned glance

Not really what you want when they're looking down there.

She tells me to get dressed

She asks how it was?

'What?'

'The . . .'

'I mean . . . every girl's first time is crap isn't it? That's what everyone says'

As if it's some kind of excuse.

As if we've all just accepted that.

'But was it, consensual?'

'What? Wh – Why?'

'Because the injuries you've sustained are . . .

What we would classify as . . .'

And my brain screams.

A montage of the **Girl***'s life starts to glitch in the background.*

A pause as the **Girl** *thinks.*

The second chorus of the song 'Come on Eileen' plays from 'That pretty red dress . . .' to '. . . tell him yes'.

I was in a car accident once.

When I was eight,

On the way to school,

A car went over a roundabout

And collided with us

I remember it happening

And just hearing a scream

This piercing feral scream

Until I realised

It was coming from me.

It's like that now

Except

No sound is coming out.

'Oh. Right. Um. Cool. It's all fine I'm sure.'

She . . . The doctor

asks how I am.

'It's exhausting, being terrified all the time . . . it sort of just blurs, till you don't even notice it anymore, it just sits under your skin, bubbling there.'

But I don't say that.

No.

I say

'OK'

Because I've learnt that being a grown-up means telling people you're OK, even when you're not.

They don't want the hassle.

Very few people want the real response to

How are you?

And that's how the most bland word in the English language was born.

'Fine . . .'

I'm fine.

Feelings

Inside

Not

Expressed

I want to ask her if they'll ever be repercussions for men who do things like this, but I think I already know the answer.

She tells me, if I want to 'talk to someone', it's a six month wait list.

And she offers me a prescription

For Prozac.

And then a lolly with a

'You're going to be okay'

If one more person

Says that resigned line.

Like there's not time

for any other option.

Like PLOT TWIST

What if I'm not?

Is that OK for you all?

Or am I dismissed

If it doesn't fit in with your schedule?

If *I am not OK.*

Nothing is OK.

There are people walking blindly around me

I'm screaming and none of you can hear.

Internally

and none of you can hear

Or see how hard I'm trying to appear

Like I am holding this together.

So just dose me up.

That's not an answer,

It's a cover up,

But we'll go with it.

I'm just tired of waking up . . .

every day.

I just want someone

To see . . .

But she stops me.

It's a

Quick fix.

For me.

For her

And she only has ten minutes per appointment

So.

Happy pills.

As I leave the doctor's

I trip over the corner of the worn out carpet

Grazing my knee.

The nurse comes over

To check I'm not going

To sue them,

And I feel the hot tears

Stream down my face.

The nurse picks me up

With a

'Come on now, you're alright'

And takes me into the triage

room

To patch me up.

She susses I'm making quite

A big fuss over a cut knee

For a sixteen-year-old.

She asks me what's wrong?

If I'm OK?

And

And

And I don't know what to say

Cos this is the first time any adult has

Asked me that.

Since . . .

She died.

So it's a shock.

And I tell her,

Everything.

About Olive,

And Mum

And Dad

And the feeling that's sat under

My skin for the past three years.

It's like someone's pulled a plug

On my brain

And it spills out on to this

Nurse whose name I don't

Even know

But she's going to have a really brilliant

Answer to

'How was your day love'

When her husband gets home.

*The **Girl** talks to the nurse.*

*The video glitches more, the **Girl** tries to block it out.*

People, uh, people, always used to tell us

How much we looked a like,

Olive would always say

'Um actually she looks like me, I was born first'

I was like her . . . mini me.

And

I'm

I'm

just

Sorry.

I'm really

Really

Sorry.

Cos . . . It was me.

It was my fault.

All of this.

And I know you'll say it's not but

But it is

It is.

I read it.

My mum left her medical file.

Out in the study.

This time we were clearing out all her stuff.

And I just want her to know that I'm sorry.

I'm sorry my existence did this to her,

But I can't,

I can't tell her.

Cos she fucking died didn't she

So

I'll never be able to tell her.

The psychiatrist said

The only reason she could decipher for

Any of this was

Me.

Cos Olive was like so smart

And so talented

And so popular

But

She wanted to look like me.

She wanted to be a small as me.

Eat all the crap I did.

The irony is I always wanted

To look like her

Be her.

The **Girl** *stands talking to the audience. 'Come on Eileen' begins to softly play in the background.*

The montage reveals photos and videos of two little girls overtaking the other montage elements.

I'm

I'm four, she's eight.

Saturday morning

Mum and Dad are still asleep

She's stolen lollies from the sweetie tin

And we're dancing on our playroom sofa.

Our matching 101 Dalmatian pyjamas flapping as we jump.

I'm three.

It's breakfast time,

No dark,

It's dark outside and

she's written, she's writing, my name in dots for me to follow and trace.

I sit on her lap and she holds my hand as she guides the pencil, as I write: Eileen and Olive. My name. Her name. Us. Connected.

Dinner time: Eileen, Olive, Eileen, Olive.

Eileen

She picked,

My name,

When I was born,

Her favourite song was 'Come on Eileen',

That's why I chose it.

For the funeral.

I was her favourite thing.

What's in a name eh?

And I realise I have blamed her

For everything.

For leaving me.

That if she'd been here.

If I'd had someone.

MY life would of turned out differently.

And I despise her in a way

You only can if you've worshipped

Someone with every ember of your being.

'And how have you, dealt with it all?'

'Hey'

The nurse is clicking at me.

'Sorry?'

'How's it all been for you?'

And I cry.

But because the whole time she was ill.

The whole six years.

No one ever asked me that.

Eileen *offers a small smile.*

Girl   I leave the doctor's

Stuffing the tablets as

Far down as they can go in my bag,

The sky feels like it needs to break

With me,

But it holds off till

I get back to Dad's and Sarah's

As I watch the rain drench the grass.

A bizarre sense of normality

Falls over me

Acceptance?

As I clock

Lottie's school bag

Under the kitchen table.

'LOTTIE'

'LOTTIE'

I must be feeling generous,

Or those tablets are working fast,

As I pound my way up the stairs.

The bathroom door's ajar

And I hear the sound of someone crying.

The kind of breathy choking crying,

When you're trying to be quiet.

I slowly open the door,

And there she sits.

On the side of the bath.

In her crumpled school uniform,

Her pony tail half fallen out,

And mascara strewn face.

I see her biro coloured hands and

note the tiny beginnings of scratches on her arms.

And my heart stops.

Fully drops to my stomach.

Because it's me.

At twelve,

The age I learnt to cry alone in bathrooms,

Because talking was dangerous,

Because I have never not seen Lottie

smile.

Because I've ignored her existence,

And this tiny slip of a girl

Wanted me.

And I wanted anyone.

But her.

I wanted mine,

My big sister,

To save me.

I catch a flash of myself in the mirror and realise

I am the age Olive was.

When she was still mine.

I recognise the fear in Lottie's eyes.

The confusion.

I've seen it in photographs

On the street,

At bus stops.

In clothes shops.

And I am so tired of that fear.

I bend down quietly,

And ask her what's wrong.

Between sniffles she finds her answer:

'It's just . . . Everything'

I tuck her hair behind her ear

And I whisper:

'Welcome to the tough years kid,

We're going to get through this'

Sensible Scout Leader Susan (*V/O*)   *Ah Eileen, I'm glad you've finally made it to the Entertainment Badge, though not a particularly talented girl, you've persevered so try to give us something worthwhile eh?*

My final badge,

I get to leave now.

It took me way too long to get them all,

But it might be the first time I've ever stuck with anything

And everyone needs something to be proud of.

Please remember that Lottie.

I'm handing the Scout baton over to you.

You wanted to know about me,

And her,

Olive.

I am now older than she ever will be.

Weird.

And you will be too one day.

I hope you can learn from my mistakes,

And make some of your own.

So . . .

You are going to hate every inch of your being

At some point.

You're going to feel so uncomfortable

You'll question your existence

And hate your parents for having you, without your permission.

The worst thing that will ever happen to you is that *you will have a feeling*. Let them in. They won't kill you. But avoiding them might

And whilst a good sense of humour will help carry you through anything

Acting like you don't care is not as cool as you think.

There will be a time where you're going to dislike how you look,

And you'll be desperate to look 'just like her'

But chances her 'just like her' wants to look 'just like you' –

We're all as self critical as each other and need a whole load of COMPASSION.

You're not missing out on anything. You don't actually want to go to that party. NO is a full sentence.

And if they don't accept your 'No' it's *thank you, next* . . .

You're going to wish

That you didn't say that comment to that boy who rolled his eyes,

Or the girls who made fun of you.

You will bump into them one day,

And smile,

Because their mean ways,

Made you stronger,

And you learnt,

Not to treat anyone that way.

Try to be kind, whenever you can,

Even when the world isn't being kind to you.

Don't beg for friendship,

Find friends, who champion each other,

The only people you owe your loyalty to, are the ones

Who never made you question theirs.

Don't respond immediately. Put the phone down. You don't need to send those texts.

Those £1.50 earrings

Will infect your ears

And if you don't look

Back at photos of yourself

And cringe

You're doing this wrong.

There will be events that leave you feeling haunted,

But the shame you're carrying around is not yours.

Acknowledge them when they appear,

And make a cup of tea.

How much you achieve has nothing

To do with what a valuable human you are,

And liking yourself is a rebellious act

So do it often.

Your are the author of your story,

Stop feeling guilty,

You're allowed to TAKE UP SPACE in the world.

A world that needs more people asking questions

Why,

How can we make this planet a better place.

But most of all,

Please remember

Even in the worst of times:

Just because the lights get turned off by circumstances outside your control, one by one, they *can* be turned back on again. By you.

Signing off, from an older

Version of you.

Who knows the very moment you are in

Right now.

And knows, you're going to be OK.

An insistent knock on her bedroom door. Lottie's voice calls 'Eileen!!'.

'Lottie, fuck off I'm busy!'

Lights down.